WHEN GOD FIRST LAUGHED

mystic poems

by

Mokasiya

Published by Mokasiya
new revised edition 2012
moon of awakening

Check out his other creations:
The Shamans' Dream
and
Climbing A Mesa (poetry from Sedona)

For poetry readings, workshops and
for additional copies of this book,
please contact Mokasiya at:
rivertink@yahoo.com
or www.rivertink.com

This book is dedicated to all that is. A day that is now unfolding when we can see, feel and know that there is no "other" and we can learn to share all resources in an awakened, unconditional, loving way.

I deeply appreciate and embrace all my relations, family and friends, who continue to teach me as I travel on this river of life.

My intention in sharing these poems is that at least one of them may reach out and touch a spark in your own heart, soul, mind, and body; that we can all explore and co-create in positive and healthy ways, this life together, on this beautiful and abundant Earth.

In Spirit, in Grace, we are all one family.
Mokasiya

WHEN GOD FIRST LAUGHED

When God
first heard
about these poems

before
they were ever written

She
began to laugh,
like a cat
purring
on my tummy.

ALL THE PIECES

In prayer
we allow
ourselves
to love

to love
all the pieces
that we are
that we feel
we are becoming

and the light
of healing
to gift
our souls.

GOD LIGHT

She
checked me out
with the God Light
illuminated
from her eyes

i was cooked
in an instant,
molded
into clay

shaped
into Her image
no longer
afraid.

REBIRTHED

Gifting love
to the sun today
with three deep breaths

i bathe my wholeness
in golden healing light

this spirit body
this physical body
this emotional body
this mindful body

i receive
the soul-ful warmth of father sun

i receive
the nurturing food of mother earth

i give love unconditionally
for the greatest good of all

i open my heart-spirit
with sun and earth
creating love together
fully re-birthed.

A SENSE OF HUMOR

I asked
what kind of God created me?

I've lied, cheated, blamed, shamed,
and attacked others

wallowed in sadness, doubt, and fear
desired people for money, power, and sex

passed judgment
searched for love outside of self

had fits and tantrums
acted out my wounded child

finally,
when I stopped all this self indulging,
moaning, and groaning
a warm silence of a breeze
whispered this answer;

what kind of God created you?

a God
with a keen sense
of humor.

MANY PATHS

All paths of the heart
lead to Spirit.

All that is Spirit
leads to unconditional love.

All unconditional love
leads to light.

All light
leads to laughter.

All laughter
leads to Spirit.

All that is Spirit
leads back
to the heart.

PEEL THE ONION

Let go
of the pain
the hair
style of illusions

come down
off the cross

peel the onion

until tears
of ecstatic joy
open your heart

now,
breathe in
breathe out

there is only
love here,
there is only
love.

MY CAREER

There are nights
i play without sleep
writing love poems
to the Divine,
then placing them
on the spokes of bicycles,
under wiper blades of cars;
attaching them
to the barbless hooks
of fishermen,
leaving them
freshly baked in the oven,
tucking them in
among the green beans,
the winter squash
and fresh clean linens,
placing them on tree branches
to be carried away
by spirit wind

i have now come to realize
i am so blessed
with such a fulfilling
vocation.

NO KEEPING SECRETS

Are we all having
a love affair
with the Beloved?

if so
shall we
keep it a secret?

it could be
contagious
and
the whole world
might join in

then
what would we do?

Ok Beloved
tickle us there
once again

so we can all
go on laughing
with God.

The Goddess Moon

Is that a flower i see
blooming endlessly
in all directions
from the center
of your heart?

then touch
the Goddess Moon
once again
with your smile

and dance
among the woodlands
wild dreams.

WHEN GODDESS LAUGHED

When Goddess
first laughed
there was no one
on this planet
to hear Her

well,
that's not
entirely true

there was
clay and water
wind and fire
earth and stone.

PLAYING HULA HOOP

This is the night
when stars
 played hula hoop
with your soul

you received
a full compass
set of directions

the winter dark air
lapped at your feet

you breathed in
the calling
of the mystery

you breathed out
simply
to love.

AN OLD DISHTOWEL

Goddess,
when you first rip-rapt your tongue
around mine
and taught me to chant
in universal sounds

i was tossed
out of the temple
and began wandering the streets
with nothing
but an old dishtowel

i have been blessed
ever since that first encounter

when you took your holy brush
and gently paint-stroked
the cells of my body

outlining a rhythm
that is love.

BACK RUBS

There were
three of us
in the bed
last night

me
the cat
and Jesus

maybe
i better not tell

but,
he gives
excellent
back rubs.

THE STUDIO

Only a small
pearl of sleep

the futon
thin
like a floating cloud

playing love tag
all night
with angels.

EVEN GOD MUST CHANGE

Can you taste the snow
in sound of wind
traveling this birth of joy
breathing inward
and onto the land?

my heart reaches out
like an avalanche of sunlight
embracing the All Maker

where even God must change
in the expansion of the soul
that touches and merges
with all that is

like a snowfield
surrendering
melting
her liquid life
into this abundantly
healing
Earth.

GAIA, EARTH GODDESS

Looking out
through the snow cloth
of white winter breath,
the cold
touched a vision
with the sacred light of Gaia
kissing the skin layers
of oak, birch and aspen

the trees
sway and moan
touched by her love

standing alone, barefoot
on snow melted edges
like a mystical deer
tasting the wind

where silence moves
erupting
into every cell
of my longing

as Gaia
tickles and anoints
these feet.

YOUR NAME

Like
a single leaf

about
to let go
of the tree

everyday
i tremble
at the calling
of your name.

SILVER SUNS

Today
out walking
i found

three
silver suns
beside the path.

To no one
i said,

"Oh my goodness!
what angels
are watching out
for me today."

THE BEST SEAT

I feel so blessed
i have the best seat in the house.
All around me is moss,
stones, trees, marsh grass,
living water of river,
the call of crows, geese and swans;
all around and all inside of me
is the essence of The Divine.

I am so blessed,
i have the best seat in the house.
Come now and sit beside me
there is more space than we can imagine,
this room has no doors, keys or locks,
all the windows are wide open
so the birds can fly through,
along with the gentle breezes
that touch the voice of our hearts.

Yes, this is the best seat in the house
to sing, play music, dance and laugh;
all that is needed
is your willingness to show up,
bring a dish to pass,
an open bowl of smiles
and a little padding
for your seat.

SWEET AND CERTAIN

When i first saw and realized
that the moon and sun
were making love
to the earth
and they asked me
to come and join them

i was nervous and uncertain

then
when they held me
like a cloud
kissing me gently

it was sweet and certain

soon
we were all having
a great
belly laugh
together.

GOD LAUGHED

When God
first laughed
playing
with my skin

our hands resembled
some exotic fruit
i had eaten
in a silent dream

where the passion
of love
wove a matrix of light
from one volcanic lip
to another

flowing into me
like water
over the sun.

START PRAYING

Is there a way to know God?

by praying
to every earthworm
that we meet

protecting the life
of every human
that may have harmed us

blessing the stones
that crawl
inside our shoes

giving thanks
to every insect
that has ever bitten us

embracing the homeless
feeding the hungry
touching the sick

then, opening our hearts
until, we begin to weep.

CRYING FOR GOD

I went into a rage
screaming curses
to the One i loved

erupting, burning, overflowing,
a flood of insanity
to all who came near

i was the Mount Saint Helens
devouring all in my path

then, an angel of the night
pulled me to the ground
placed me in a headlock
while i kicked, screamed,
moaning at the mouth

this angel held me
until all the craziness
melted away
inside of me

and then i walked,
slowly in the dark,
crying for her return.

GURU YOGA

Naropa realized
the natural state of Being
when his teacher, unexpectedly,
struck him on the forehead
with his sandal

Nagabodhi attained
supreme accomplishment
by eating a piece of snot
dropped by noble master, Nagarjuna

For some of us
it may be better
to eat yak dung for a day
then to read
all the volumes
of holy scriptures

Enlightenment,
perhaps,
is a simple sound
that everyone can embrace
from within.
om mani padmi om.

GAVE BIRTH

Next to Her
in the deepening quick

where Spring
gave birth
to moss
and flower.

CENTERING

Centered in joy
centered in love

centered in truth
centered in prayer

centered in breath
centered in oneness

Winter
is centering in.

TASTING GOD

When i first
felt your playfulness
upon my tongue

and i opened my mouth
in prayer
to receive you

nothing mystical
really happened

still, i thought
to build a shrine
in your honor

you only smiled then
and simply advised

"better to go
and gather wild nuts
and ripe berries
in the forest

then
you can taste me
again and again."

FILLING THE DAYS

I asked God,
how could you be
such a jerk, such a zealot,
allowing all these diseases,
wars, famines to go on in the world?

some days
i am really pissed off at you

it is just like you Dear One
not to respond to this question

"Your question
is more like an attack,
is it not the thoughts in your mind
that has created me
to be a jerk, a zealot, a judging God
that has allowed war, disease and
hunger to go on in the world?

come closer to my lips
and I will hold you now
so the illusions in your mind
can all drift away
and the light in your heart
can fill the days
with miracles, unity and joy."

IN THE MIDDLE

In the middle
of nothing
　　　is everything

in the center
of awareness
　　　is your soul

in the awakening
from the dream
　　　is your freedom.

Going So Far

So far
how is the deep
conscious awareness
working for you

more pain, suffering
or betrayal?

try the unconscious life
for a moment

and just maybe
you will breathe
the Holy Grail,
the Divine Laughter
of your soul.

RECEIVING A SACRAMENT

Would it be wise
to meet on another day
when the dark side of illusion, anger,
and conquest become a gift to heal

let's feed our love
rather than our wounded
vacuum of fear

and witness one another
out in the forest,
where we can weep and scream
until the blood in our veins
sinks into our hearts

until our voices grow numb and silent
melting into the earth
into the womb mother
filling her soul
with the fountain of our souls

let's remember to breathe
chew on some leaves, twigs, and dirt
possibly an earthworm
may crawl upon our backs
whispering in our ears
the sacrament of love.

A LAUGHING GOD

When God cried
for what seemed
like endless time
in the days and weeks
of thick darkness

the great oceans were formed

one day
when the blazing orb of sun
decided to appear,
that's when God
first laughed
and out of Her mouth
all forms of life were created

is that why
all that we now see
is Sacred?

SHARE YOUR GIFTS

Last night
the moon
tilted on its side
half full of light
with a voice that said
"I am open,
come
play along my golden ridges,
curves, hollows and mountaintops
there is more than enough room for all
on the floor of this launching pad,
to spin and laugh
transforming all your dreams."

"come now
fill your cup
with such sweet nectar,
on a night like this
nestle close beside me,
and open
those boxes of chocolates
sharing your gifts
to all you encounter,
with a clear, loving mind
and an opened
kind heart."

HOW TO PRAY

Fold
all your love letters
all your love poems
into the shapes
of birds

then blow
on each one
gently
with your breath
and release them
into the mystic
night air

i know
of no better way
to pray.

SWEET POTATO

You will never
convince me
that there is a God.

You will never
convince me
that there is anything but God.

So let's take a risk
and share this hot
Sweet Potato
without the need
of fork, knife or spoon

and with our tummies full
paint love patterns
in the soft belly sky
with the holy bones
of our finger-tips,
with the holy bones
of our finger-tips.

JUST A SUGGESTION

Do you truly
want union
with the divine?

then begin
by writing
your own song

singing
your own prayers

dancing
in the forest

splashing
your holy feet
in a puddle

and listening
deeply
in early morning
to the calling
of birds.

SACRED LOVE

I'm sorry
what did you say?

i am not here to convince you
that there is a male or female God,
a single God, a married God,
a divorced God, a loving God,
a vengeful God, ten billion Gods,
one God or no God

so please relax your mind
place all your skin colors
next to the Mystical One

peel away layers of self-doubt
toss them into the blue flame
of earth and holy spirit
then wrap your softness
all around your loving soul

touching hearts
with the moist petals of raindrops,
kissing all again and again
with the nectarine of your breath

i'm sorry
i'm not here
to convince you
of anything

when a simple bubble
of the Wanderer
touches your forehead
and your feet begin
to teach you
how to dance and spin

then go ahead
fill all your pots and pans
with a great stew
there are many
hungry mouths to feed
with the ladle
of Sacred Love.

BELLY BUTTONS

Two belly buttons
one a crater
the other an eye

when Universe blinked
they became the eyes
of the Creator's
crater.

40

FORTUNATELY

Once
i had a thought
that i really, really
knew something

fortunately
i quickly forgot
what it was.

SATORI

Today, we are sitting
on our Satori*
gazing at the mind
a bone yard
of half-stripped car parts
rusting in the weeds

always recycled
in the silence
of sun
rain
wind
and snow

all those personalities
disassembled
piece by peace

until what is left
is crushed
hauled off
then melted
into God.

*Satori
sudden enlightenment

WHO IS EMPTY

I am so empty
i am filled
with abundance

i am so dead
i can no longer die

i am so much
like myself
i do not know
who i am

i am so angry
that my rage
dissolves into laughter

with Spirit
i am whole

with God
i begin
to taste love.

WE LAUGHED

When i first saw God
we both laughed,

is it best
i do not tell
what we really did?

some intimate details
are not always ready
to be shared.

TEACH ME

Goddess
Divine One

teach me

for this head
is a vacant lot.

KISSING THE HUNGRY ONES

The moon is full
of mischievous acts tonight

performing
open heart surgery
upon our chests

seeking its own vision
with enchanted lovers

calling the owls
whippoorwills
nightingales
that sing into all hearts

She never had to floss
like the rest of us

or decide
what kind of clothes to wear

once i saw Her
dip underneath the clouds

kissing, all the hungry ones
on the forehead.

46

BEAUTY IS

There is the rain

the dream
about the rain

the dreamer
who dreamed the rain

the trees
that sang to the clouds
"come,
quench our loving thirst"

and taste this world
suspended
in a single raindrop
on the bee pollen stamen
of a wild rose

beauty
is fragile like this

beauty
is holy and complete
like this.

SPIRITUAL UNION

Even then
when rivers wept
across the room
of painted drums
and ten thousand angels sang

Glory Be!

to their love union
born
not only of the flesh
but from
the Sacred Heart Mystery
that nurtures
all souls.

AN OFFERING

I feel
a poem

spinning

on the edge
of my lip

when we kissed
it was offered
into God.

MAKING MUD PIES

The first time
i saw a horse pee
i couldn't believe my eyes

the first time
i made love with God
i felt like a child
making mud pies
in a sandbox

what do
these two experiences
have in common

nothing really
except,
they both
made God
laugh.

PLAYING RING TOSS

Do you know the Beloved?

Have you glimpsed the radiance
of the Dear One
inside your heart?

Have you opened all the shop windows
to The Joyful One
who dances wild in the streets?

Have you kept the night light burning
in your soul
so the Sweet One
can find a way home?

Have you emptied the torrent
from your mind
so the Divine
can fill all your thoughts
with love?

Can you start now
by gently playing ring toss
with the moon
and celebrate your love
with ambrosia, sage and sweet grass?

TO SURRENDER

What is that
we are touching
underneath the sheath
of this body?

is this God, loving God
praying at our elbows

gently pouring
sweet jasmine tea
into our open pores

our eyes
removing the nightgown
veil of fear

underneath the mask
the nectar of wetness
moves into us

then, the quickening
the healing joy begins

and we only need
now, to surrender.

THIS DESSERT

Oh Dear One!
how can i explain this
the way you dance
in such complete bliss
with all that you touch
day after day

no expectations
guilt, blame or shame
no pain
although, you might be cautious
about exposing yourself too long
sun burning your skin

this unconditional love
goes on every moment
it's been happening
for millions of years

go ahead, dip your spoon
into this dessert

there is more than enough
to go around
again and again
for everyone.

FLOWERS

Kissed by sun
moon
wind
rain

each bloom
speaks
a thousand languages

touched
by human hands,
they pulsate
the colors
of our hearts

and open
their love
upon the windowsills
of our longing.

HEARING GOD LAUGH

When i first heard
God laugh

i thought
it was the wind
talking
to the trees

then, i thought
it was the night, ocean surf
singing to the moon

then, i realized
it was both of these
and more,
like The Lover
whispering joy
into all souls.

UNION

God,
you no longer need
to hold back
or be afraid
to come close to me

i am a vessel
no longer waiting
to be filled
with your love

i am a ripened fruit
opening to feed the hungry

i am a spring of pure water
here, to quench your thirst

i am light
pulsating
uniting
with your Soul.

WHAT ELSE

My friend
once said
to a bee

"what
did you do
today?"

and the bee replied,
"i flew
among the flowers
gently
pressing
my tongue
into each
opened petal

what else
could i possibly do
for God today?"

RENEWAL

It was simply
the wave
of the moon,
close
intimate
foaming around my knees
ankles
feet
and thighs

so close
i could stretch
into its cantaloupe brightness

and renew
the tenderness
the completeness
of my soul.

HEARTS WILL OPEN

When there is
nothing
to fear

nothing
to remember

nothing
to explain

eyes
will meet

hearts
will open

and be touched
in the moment
of the Beloved.

A BITE FROM THE DIVINE

You have done it now
filled all my pores
with your crystal light

you want me to share this
with the world?
what lovers
we have become
oozing with your kindness

so bite me now
gently
and massage
my soul.

LIGHTIN' UP

After
you called
i sat
inside the moon

until
She spilled me out
into the tide
of the land

where i
became a human
in the light
that i am.

A RISK

For just one moment
if you touched
the clear glass of me
to your lips

with all your will
all your awareness
all your intention

and swallowed
the water
of my soul
into yours

we could transform
this moment, this life-time

it's a risk

so,
what else
is new?

AN OPENED SACK

The One
who never seems
to clean up
after himself

awoke me
in the night

crawled
into my bed

laughing, laughing

then tickling me
in that
loving sweet way
with an opened sack
full of stars.

SPIRIT

It dips
out of a cloud
of nothingness

and awakens
our souls

like
      sunlight
in   *****
      water
            ≈≈≈≈

BREATHE

Breathe
me now
like a rose

in this moment
when our lips
clearly touch

and the mind reposes
like the song
of a thrush.

Author's note

What can be said about God and Goddess?
That it comes from inside each one of us?
As long as there are sentient beings, on this
Earth, I imagine there to be a growing
consciousness about, "The Great Mystery."
For now, what do we pray about, hold onto, and
let go of, in sharing our many ideas and beliefs,
about the unknown and the unknowable?
May we all learn to listen well, speak with a
gentle smile, a playful mind, and a kind and
loving heart.

peace,
Mokasiya

Made in the USA
Lexington, KY
15 February 2013